**CIRCULATING WITH THE LISTED PROBLEM(S):**

stain A/H 10-22-01

**DO NOT REMOVE**
**CARDS FROM POCKET**

This book is dedicated
to my mother, Dorothy Saunders,
who taught me the joy of making things
and to my family, Bob, Betsy and Sarah,
who encourage me to continue

# Bulletin Boards and Displays

*Good Ideas for Librarians and Teachers*

*by*
Gayle Skaggs

McFarland & Company, Inc., Publishers
*Jefferson, North Carolina, and London*

British Library Cataloguing-in-Publication data are available

Library of Congress Cataloguing-in-Publication Data

Skaggs, Gayle, 1952–
    Bulletin boards and displays : good ideas for librarians and
teachers / by Gayle Skaggs.
        p.  cm.
    Includes index.
    ISBN 0-89950-884-7 (sewn softcover : 55# alk. paper) ∞
    1. School libraries—United States.  2. Library exhibits—United
States.  3. Displays in education.  4. Bulletin boards.  I. Title.
Z675.S3S597   1993
027.8'223'0973—dc20                                    92-56694
                                                            CIP

Manufactured in the United States of America

*McFarland & Company, Inc., Publishers*
  *Box 611, Jefferson, North Carolina 28640*

# Contents

# Introduction

Facing the challenge of creating a new library bulletin board or display is often the cause of an anxiety attack. Where can one find an idea that is modern enough to appeal to today's secondary school student and also one that relates to the use of the library? This book is designed to present some ideas that are not all original but have been used successfully in a secondary school library setting. These bulletin boards and displays could be used just as presented or might be a springboard for your own ideas and creativity.

Television shows are also great fun for ideas. Incorporate a game show title into the bulletin board message such as "Wheel of Fortune." This can easily be changed to "Wheel of Good Fortune."

## Go for a Spin on Your Library's Wheel of Good Fortune

Think of this as two circles—a small one on top of a larger circle. Use poster board, heavy paper or cardboard to create the two circles. (See illustration on page viii.)

Make a pattern for the smallest circle out of newspaper. Divide this newspaper circle into twelve pieces to use as a pattern to mark the poster board. If different colors for each Dewey classification are desired, use the pattern to cut the correct size piece and glue it on a heavy circle backing.

Use a metal brad in the center which goes through both circles. This will allow the circles to actually turn.

Use a black marker to label the pieces or cut the letters from construction paper. Use any color letters to finish up the display.

There are many ideas that can be repeated year after year, at any time of the year. How about a king-size calendar for the month? Fill in all the usual important information but add little extras that are special to your students like ball games, dances and other events. A small amount of research will yield those off-the-wall events like National Pickle Day or Elvis' birthday. Researching the days could be done by your students or become part of a contest. Calendars do not have to be in the traditional form. Be different! Try a continuous line or even use your school's initials.

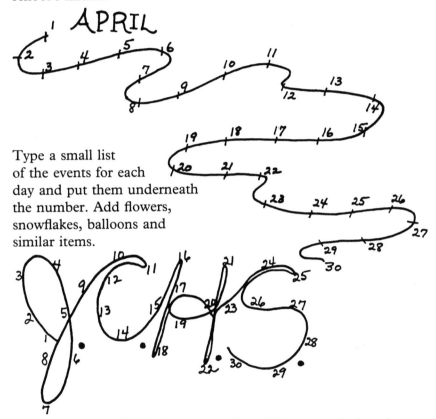

Type a small list of the events for each day and put them underneath the number. Add flowers, snowflakes, balloons and similar items.

Another possibility is to use prints of famous paintings but add words as though the painting could talk. Type words on white paper and create comic book–style balloons. Center all the words around reading. For example:

> *"A good book cracks me up!"* Use this with a portrait of George Washington.

> *"Honest, I turned in that book!"* Use this with a portrait of Abraham Lincoln.

This idea can be used over and over just by changing the art prints or the words. Photographs of famous people such as politicians in election years or sports heroes are just as effective.

The possibilities are endless. Your bulletin boards will become a popular and important part of your library if you change them frequently and strive to keep up with the times with relevant themes and a little creativity.

What type of display area do you have to work with? If your bulletin board is small, why not go beyond the borders and use an entire wall? Masking tape works wonders and, if used carefully, will not damage the paint. (Test a small area before creating a large display.) Change the size frequently and keep your audience guessing.

Begin to view your space from all angles. Is it possible for you to also utilize the ceiling directly in front of the bulletin

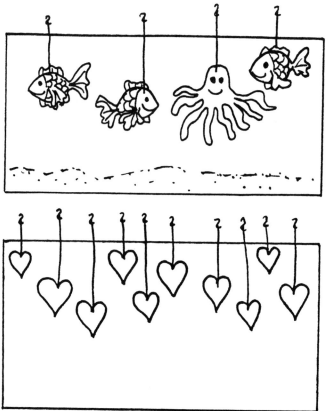

board? By hanging objects from the ceiling such as hearts, fish, or just book jackets, the effect will then become more three-dimensional. This allows the viewer to walk through the display and become part of it.

Fishing line is terrific for hanging objects. It is clear, very strong and inexpensive. A paper clip pulled apart makes a great hook to attach to a light figure or fit into the seam of a ceiling tile.

Just as recycling is important ecologically, it is equally important as far as bulletin boards and displays are concerned. Save all of the pieces of every bulletin board by placing them on a sturdy piece of cardboard in large labeled trash bags or envelopes. Protecting the construction paper from unnecessary sunlight will extend the life of each item. It is a good idea to draw a small sketch of the finished product so that it would be possible to reassemble the display a second time. It is often possible to create new and exciting displays by using bits and pieces of previous displays. Be smart and look for every opportunity to recycle.

## Part I
# The Basics

*The Background*

One of the primary things to consider as you plan your bulletin board is the type of background to use. You are only limited by your imagination. Even on the strictest budget, it is possible to use creative backgrounds. Listed below are some possibilities:

• Construction paper.
• Newspaper—*The Wall Street Journal* is especially nice as a background; or be bolder and use the comics section.
• Old sheets—dye an old white sheet blue for an outdoor background or try tie-dye for an unusual effect. Become really fancy and applique a background using a sheet and bits of fabric.
• Wallpaper—use leftover rolls or use samples from wallpaper books.
• Wrapping paper.
• Brown mailing paper.
• Burlap or material remnants.
• Colored poster paper on a roll. This is available in a large variety of colors.
• Butcher paper or newsprint. End rolls are often available at the local newspaper free of charge.
• Pages from old magazines or old telephone books.

- Sheets of corrugated cardboard.
- Rolls of batting (the material inside a quilt) for a snow effect.
- Old quilts or bedspreads.
- Paper tablecloth.
- Black plastic trash bags opened up.

Be wise in your color choices. The colors you choose can set the mood of the display with bright, vivid colors being attention-getters. Vary the colors, just as everything else, so as not to tire your audience. Remember that fresh clean paper evokes a more positive response than a faded old paper, used and reused.

## Visuals

If you do not feel confident in drawing or creating visuals for the bulletin board, try using an opaque projector to enlarge pictures from books, newspapers, or magazines. These can easily be traced and will look professionally done.

If your school has a mascot, plan to use it as often as feasible. Using this symbol and featuring your school's colors helps to personalize your displays.

## The Border

Another important component is the border. A border's function is to finish up the edges and form the boundary of the display area. The border helps to draw the viewer's eye to the display and supports the general theme.

Borders can be made from any material and can be as simple as just using book covers. Symbols of any kind can be used such as hearts, arrows or exclamation marks. The following is a basic list of a few border possibilities:

- Purchased borders—commercially produced.

•Rope.

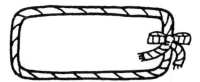

• Net.

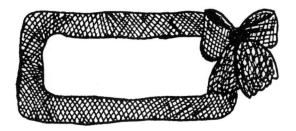

• Cut arrows (or any other symbol) from construction paper or poster board to symbolize action.

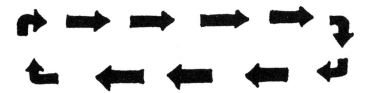

• Use footprints for a mystery or detective display.

• Desk-top publishing programs often have borders that can be used for ideas.

- Yellow circles simulate light bulbs for showcasing your patrons. This gives the feeling of a star's dressing room mirror.

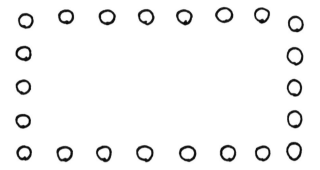

## *The Lettering*

The message of your bulletin board or display should be in clear, easy-to-read letters. Keep it simple. People do not usually spend a large amount of time studying a bulletin board, so it must be designed to be easily understood. Strive to make the display as professional as possible.

Just as the type of background should vary from time to time, so should the style of letters used. This can be done by changing the fonts, or letter styles, or by the materials used to create the letters. Some possibilities are listed below:

- The most common is to use standard purchased cardboard patterns to design the letters from construction paper. These are available in many styles and sizes.
- Use computer-generated letters. These are great for banners or labels. The *Print Shop* is just one of many great time savers when designing the message of your display.

• Use a long piece of net, rope, yarn, heavy string, or cotton batting and shape it into cursive letters with the help of straight pins.

• Cut letters from cardboard or poster board and then cover these with foil, wrapping paper, fabric, glitter or any material you have readily available.

• Use wallpaper. Sample wallpaper books are often available for the asking at wallpaper stores.

• Try puffy letters. These can be easily made by cutting two of the same shape letters out of paper. These two shapes are then stapled together and are stuffed with small pieces of newspaper. These letters can also be made from fabric and stuffed with fiberfill.

• Write the message in cursive. Widen the lines to give space to cut out the words.

# Part II
# Bulletin Board Ideas

The following pages contain sixty-five tried-and-true ideas for library bulletin boards. Use them as they are or expand and improve them with your own ideas. The bulletin board becomes an extension of you and your enthusiasm for the library and reading. Go for it!

Exact sizes of paper and other items are not given. The intent of this book is to offer ideas and suggestions, not necessarily bulletin board kits. It is important that you make the idea fit into your specific surroundings.

Please note that many of the following bulletin boards use book covers as part of the total design. If you do not have access to book covers, make your own or use old magazine covers or newspapers. Sponsor a contest among your students to create special book jackets. This will not only help you but will spark extra enthusiasm about your library displays. Each idea is usable even without the book covers. Use what you have available.

The mascot for my high school is Jasper, a red jaybird. He will appear in several of the designs. Substitute your school's mascot to create as personal a display as possible.

# START THE YEAR ON THE RIGHT FOOT

This can be used anywhere and done in any size. It was originally designed to be used floor-to-ceiling and the enormous size was a definite attention-getter.

Construct the legs and shoes from construction paper. Outline the edges of everything with a dark marker. This gives it a more finished look and draws more attention.

Finish the display with any style of lettering.

To carry the "right foot" theme throughout the library, use old shoes (always the right shoe only) to display paperbacks, artificial flowers or even a small plant in an old tennis shoe. The rubber sole will hold the water fairly well.

Start the year on the right foot. **READ!**

# WELCOME  BACK

This would be best for a junior high or elementary bulletin board. This whole display can be any size from small all the way to full wall size.

Start with the big, yellow bus. Think of the bus as a large oval.

Make a front for the bus. Add two black construction paper circles for tires. Use a smaller circle for the hubcap.

Cut out windows. Make the smiling faces out of construction paper and use markers for the details. Consider using your school mascot for the driver.

Your school's name belongs here

This can be bright and cheerful and a great way to welcome back your students.

# HAVE A TREE-MENDOUS YEAR!

Use any color plain background. Make a tree from construction paper or on cardboard. Make it from something sturdy so that it can be used and reused.

Cut construction paper leaves in bright fall colors. Alternate book covers and leaves around the tree. Student-written book reviews could be substituted for the book covers. Fold the leaves and pin them on so that they stick out a little for a more interesting effect.

Use dark letters for the message.

An appropriate border could be made from cut leaves. Real leaves may be used if pressed for several days in a heavy book or leaf press.

# RESEARCH PROBLEMS?

This is a very flexible display. It can be made any size and shape and works just as well horizontally as vertically.

Make a pattern for the hands by tracing one of your hands. Choose any combination of three or four colors of construction paper and trace the pattern. Turn the pattern over every once in a while so that you will have both right and left hands. Cut these out and use them for the border.

Use black or bold blue for the letters.

Additional hands can be used with a book display to carry the theme throughout the library.

Research Problems? Let The Librarians Give You A Hand.

# PUZZLED ABOUT THE LIBRARY?

Cut construction paper into large puzzle pieces. Use a marker to write on the questions you are most often asked. This is good to use early in the school year to answer those questions right away.

You might also want to consider including the answers.

# PUZZLED BY THE LIBRARY?

Create a library crossword puzzle yourself or use the *Crossword Magic* computer program. Think of words relating to the library to incorporate into a puzzle. This idea can also be used to feature the names of authors, special events and other themes.

If your display space is large enough, make each square 6"×6". Cut an 18" strip of construction paper and divide it into 6" squares. Outline the squares in black marker.

These squares can be cut apart or used in 3s as needed.

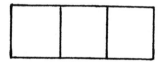

Use computer generated signs for the clues, one for each. Spread the clues out. These are bunched up due to limited page space.

This is not particularly the best text for the bulletin board. Actually the puzzle will speak for itself with no extra text needed at all.

A crossword puzzle done on a large scale personalized to fit your library and school will be well received. Your patrons will marvel at what appears to be a highly complex design problem when in actuality, it was a snap to make!

# PUZZLED BY THE LIBRARY? ASK QUESTIONS...

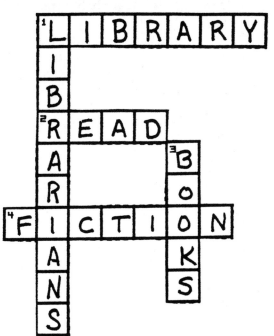

## ACROSS

1. The special place in school where books, videos, magazines, etc. are housed.
2. A great activity to do anytime.
4. Stories that are not true.

## DOWN

1. The friendly helpful people who work in the library.
3. Information that can be fiction or non-fiction.

# PUZZLED BY WORLD EVENTS?

This is a simple bulletin board but one that can cause a great many comments. Many patrons will be horrified by the fact that the map was cut up while the majority will really think it is graphically appealing. (This was probably one of my most popular bulletin boards!)

Take a colorful world map and cut it into five or six puzzle pieces. Use a bold color of construction paper to complement your puzzle pieces and serve as the background. Spread out the puzzle pieces in the display. Mix them up.

Use dark letters for the message.

The whole display will take virtually no time to make and will work effectively on any shape bulletin board.

# WHERE IN THE WORLD IS?

This works well as a display that changes daily or at least frequently. Change the locations to keep your patrons searching for those out-of-the-way spots. This would be great to use during National Geography Week. It could be brought to a different level by using your state map or even a map of your county.

This will not require much advanced preparation but the interest level will be maintained by the new addition of hard-to-find locations. Use a world map as the background.

Print the locations you choose to feature on a strip of construction paper or poster board for ease in movement. You might point out each spot before moving on to the next one. This can be done by stretching a piece of string or yarn from the actual location on the map to the strip of paper.

# Where In The World Is?

Canberra

Cancun

Madagascar

Guam

Togo

Kenya

St. Lucia

# MASTERPIECES OF LITERATURE

Use three different colors of construction paper, each sheet 12×18 (or 18×24) depending upon the size of your display area.

Cut each sheet into two puzzle pieces.

Choose six books which you feel students should read. You will use one of these puzzle pieces for each book.

There are several ways to do these puzzle pieces. One suggestion would be to use colored chalk or markers to write the title. Colored chalk can be used around the edges to soften them. Use two colors of chalk and blend them together with your finger. They will smear together on the page giving a great effect. When you are finished with the chalk drawing, spray it with a fixative to prevent future smearing. Cheap hairspray works well as a fixative.

If you have book jackets for these six books, they could be used.

You could ask six different students to design one piece. The word "masterpiece" will then mean several different things. It is terrific to involve your students as often as possible in the display process.

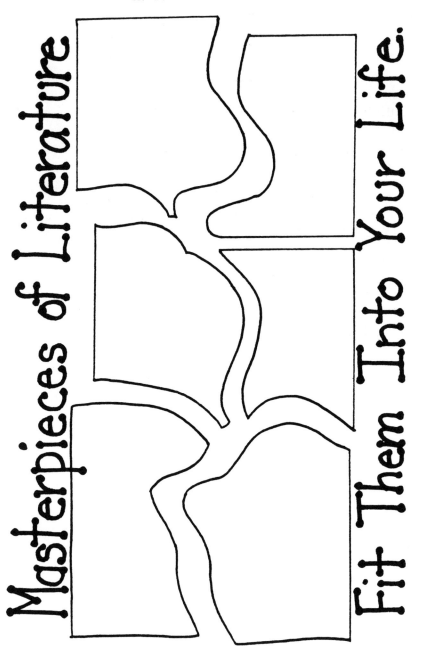

Masterpieces of Literature

Fit Them Into Your Life.

# WE AIM TO PLEASE

Cut a large, bright circle out of poster board or construction paper. Cut four smaller circles as shown in the design. A different bright color for each circle would be most effective. Glue the circles together to form a bull's-eye target design. Use a dark marker to draw in the letter grades or cut them from construction paper.

The arrow should be made from construction paper but use fluffed-out yarn or narrow strips of paper for the feathers.

Any style of letters is appropriate. No particular background is required.

# LET US HELP YOU SHOOT
# FOR HIGHER GRADES.

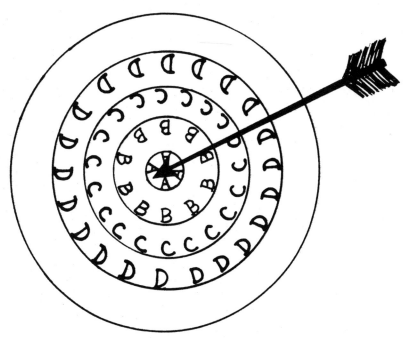

# WE AIM TO PLEASE.

# "EWE" WILL LOVE OUR NEW BOOKS

Sheep are very popular these days. This particular idea won't take any time at all to make. Keep it as simple as possible.

Use a light, bright background so that your sheep will really stand out. Use a whole flock and spread them throughout the library.

The sheep's body could be made from white construction paper or poster board. This can be used as is or glue on polyester fiberfill or cotton balls to achieve a more three-dimensional, fluffy look.

Use black paper or poster board for the face, ears and legs.

Finish up the display with book covers, book reviews or even student-designed book covers and add a fence for an appropriate border.

**Ear**  cut one and fold it down the middle to make it stand out.

**Legs**  cut four identical rectangles. Cut a small V-shape on one end of each rectangle to form the feet. Glue legs into place.

**Face**  cut an oval shape. Only half of the oval will show. The remaining half will be glued behind the white paper of the head.

**Body** cut a cloud-like shape from the white paper or poster board.

"Ewe" Will Love Our New Books.

# DON'T WORRY

This is good if you need a quick display. Use your school mascot and school colors. Keep everything very simple.

Don't worry... it will work.

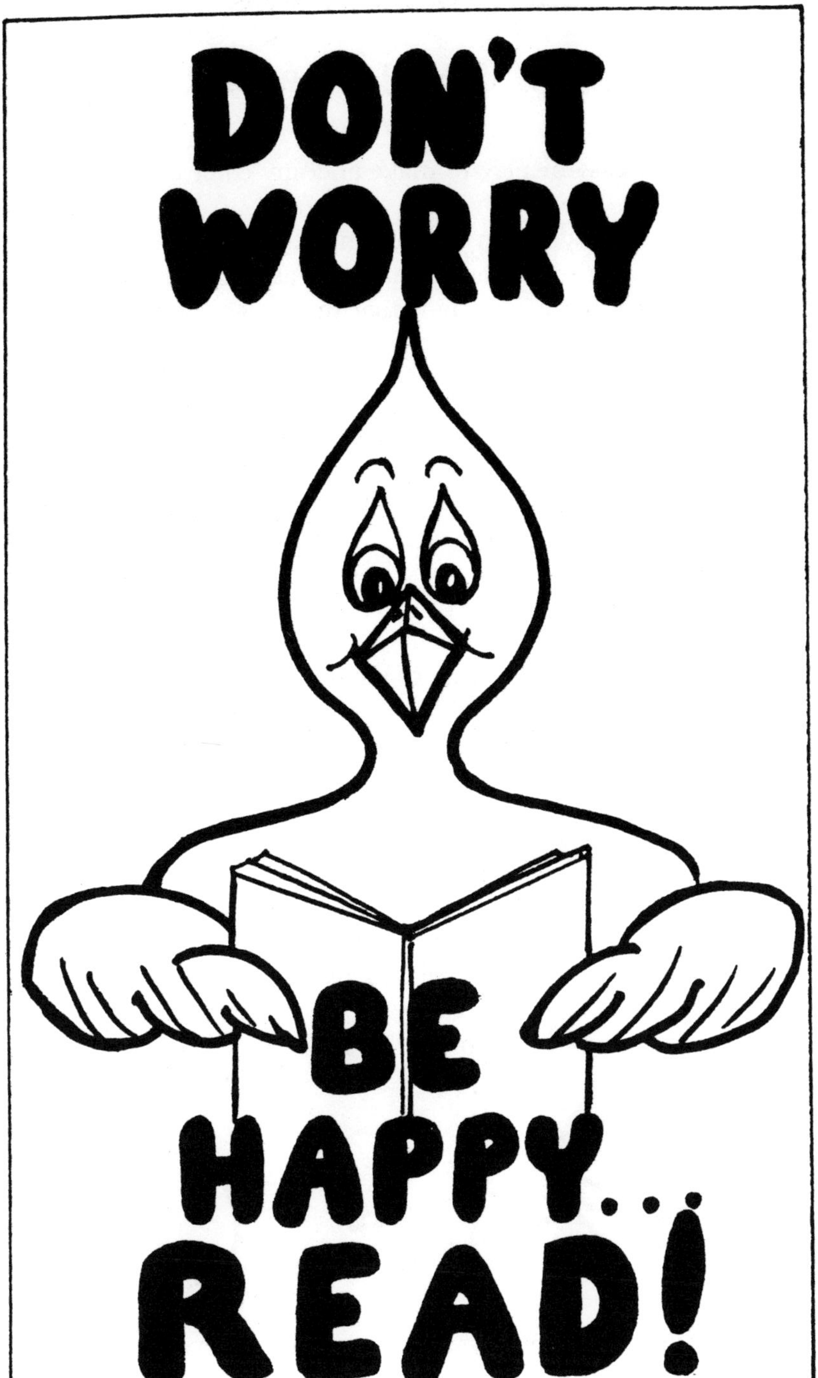
DON'T
WORRY
BE
HAPPY...
READ!

# GIVE YOURSELF A TREAT

This is an easy display to make and any color combinations will work.

For the treats, you can cut out any yummy-looking goodies from magazines or make them yourself. Fast food restaurants might have some appealing signs that they might donate to you. A soft drink cup could be cut in half lengthwise and pinned on. Fasten a couple of real straws in it with tape.

For the candy, cut a circle of any color construction paper or poster board and use a marker to create the spiral design. Use a stick or a piece of brown construction paper for the lollipop stick.

Wrap the candy in clear cellophane or plastic wrap to give it a more finished look. Other candy pieces can be made by using construction paper and the plastic wrap.

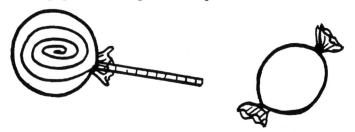

Add some book covers, magazine covers or even a newspaper to finish up the display.

# HATS OFF TO READING

This display can be adjusted to any size. Use a plain background and use real hats of varying sizes. Unusual hats will attract the most attention but security might be a problem. Pin the hats on in various places to feature book jackets. Hats could even be hung from the ceiling directly in front of the bulletin board to give the appearance that the wind has really blown in some hats from somewhere.

Use dark letters to present your message.

# HOLD ON TO YOUR HAT!

Any background, size or shape will work for this super-simple display. Use large letters for all the words. This is supposed to be an exclamation!

Use an assortment of real hats pinned on in various poses and include a hand or two with each one. Trace around your hand to make a pattern and then cut the hands out of construction paper.

Book covers are not necessary. This is basically an informative display to call attention to your new books.

HOLD ON TO TO YOUR HAT!
THE NEW BOOKS ARE HERE!

# SPY OUT SOME
# OF OUR NEW BOOKS

Make your spies out of black poster board or heavy construction paper. Save these for future use. They fit in for all types of mystery displays. Just cut out the black in one piece and glue on the eyes, nose and hands. These spies could be made any size.

Use book jackets, any type of background, and any style letters to complete the display. Footprints work well as a border. The spy theme is accentuated by the use of a magnifying glass and a spy camera.

# ✓ OUT OUR MAGAZINES!

Use old *Wall Street Journals* for your background. Use the little spies as previously described but have them searching out old magazine covers this time. You might add another line telling your magazine check-out policy.

# READ PERIODICALLY

This can be done in several ways. For a display that is not intended to be up long, use real helium-filled balloons labeled with the names of current magazines. A marker can be used to do this.

If you desire something a little more lasting, use old magazine covers cut into as large a balloon shape as possible. Use string or yarn to tie the balloons. Use extra to have plenty to hang down around the letters. Drape the string through the letters.

Use a solid color background so as not to detract from the balloons.

Another variation would be to tie the balloons to the letters.

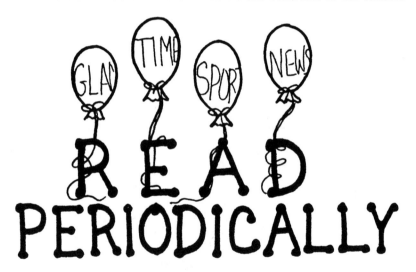

# IT CAN BE A
# JUNGLE OUT THERE

This bulletin board can be as simple or as complicated as you want it to be. Start with a blue background. Either paint or use construction paper for the foliage. Leaves and vines of any shape will work. Make a lot of whatever you make. Bright, cheerful flowers, scary snakes, butterflies, spiders, and the like can be made from construction paper. All these will add that extra touch.

The person is really only a head with a hat, one arm with hand and just a hand. Use pink construction paper for the flesh tone and any color for the hat. Use a marker for the details. Your school mascot could be used instead.

Add books covers, magazine covers, newspapers or any library-use tips.

Recycle all the pieces and use them over and over.

The bright colors are very attention-getting and the compliments will flow.

FOLIAGE                              PERSON

Choose a shape and just repeat it over and over. A heart shape works well for large leaves.

Use dark construction paper for the body and pink for the head and hands.

# DON'T GET LOST IN
# THE TERM PAPER JUNGLE

Recycle all the materials from "It Can Be a Jungle Out There" bulletin board or follow the instructions given for that design.

This particular bulletin board stresses the use of reference tools. Make a list of the most important reference tools available in your library. Add the names of these tools throughout the foliage.

# GET HUNG UP ON READING

This is a great, super-fast, no-frills display idea. This plan works well on a bulletin board or just hanging up high in a section of your library.

You will need a clothesline rope as long as the display space. If on a bulletin board, just tack the ends on either side. Otherwise, tie the ends around support posts or to anything substantial up high enough to not interfere with the traffic flow.

If space allows, use real articles of clothing such as school T-shirts, sweatshirts, shorts, even add some mismatched socks for effect. Hang these with clothespins.

Use straight pins or tape to attach book covers or magazine covers to the pieces of clothing or just clothespin them directly on the line.

Add your message in the same way. On a bulletin board, you can put the lettering above and below the line.

# HAVE A BOOK AND A SMILE!

This is a simple idea to add some humor to your library. Cut a large circle for the head. Use markers to add the features.

Make a large, oversized book or use a book jacket. Add two hands and some bold, dark letters. Keep the whole design very simple.

Display humorous books of poetry, essays, short stories and jokes throughout your library. Smile and enjoy your patrons!

# Have A Book

Jokes & Riddles

# And A SMILE!

# OVERHEARD IN THE LIBRARY

Choose prints of famous paintings, portraits of politicians, sports heroes and others. Mount them on a contrasting color of construction paper to create a framed appearance.

Using comic book–style balloons, add words as though the pictures could talk. Center all the words around reading.

"A good book cracks me up!"—George Washington

"Honest I turned in that book!"—Abraham Lincoln

"Reading *Seventeen* magazine keeps me looking beautiful."—Mona Lisa

"I'd rather be reading."

"Reading really turns me on!"

"There are 70 million books in American libraries and the one I want is always checked out."

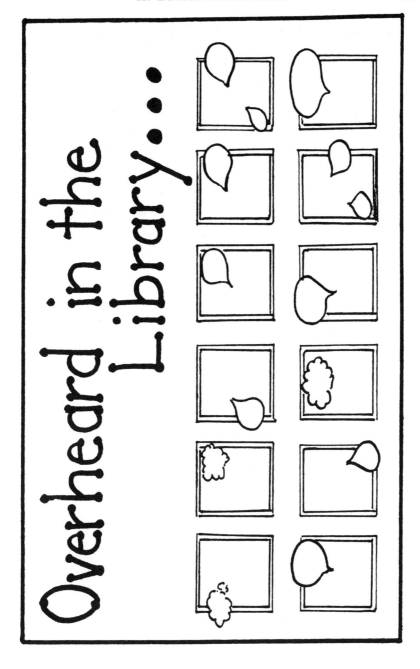

# YOUR LIBRARY...
# THE INFORMATION PLACE

This works well if you have a long, narrow, horizontal display area. Use all types of media in your letters. A record can be made from construction paper while a withdrawn filmstrip can be used along with magazine covers, newspapers and such. This is an opportunity to show off all your library's media.

Make sure that part of the letters are all the same color, preferably black, to add continuity and to aid in easily reading the message.

No particular background is necessary.

# FIND YOUR FANTASY

Use your imagination to create a dreamy effect. Blues and purples are good fantasy colors.

Use polyester fiberfill or cotton batting for the low clouds. Use white paper or poster board for those clouds in the sky. This will make the lower ones seem much closer.

This castle could be made of aluminum foil, construction paper or even from brown wrapping paper. The castle is just two rectangles the same size and another slightly shorter rectangle in the middle.

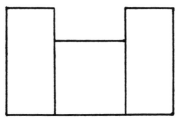

Glue the three rectangles together.

Cut out squares across the tops of the rectangles to create the towers for your castle. Cut a large doorway or glue on a doorway in a contrasting color. Use a marker to create brickwork around the door.

Add a few colorful pennants and use some fancy lettering to finish up the display.

Carry out the theme throughout the library with books on wizards, dragons and knights.

Find Your Fantasy

Read

# READ ABOUT THE MOOOVIES

The more bizarre the better for this display. Cut out pictures of cows from magazines, use real photographs you've taken or make your own ridiculous black and white cow.

Almost everyone likes to go to the movies so this idea gives you the opportunity to display movie tie-ins or books about the movie business and the big stars.

To make a cow, start with the body. Use a large sheet of black paper. Cut a large hill-shaped piece and then add some white shapes to make your cow become spotted. For the head, use a long rectangle of black construction paper. Round off the corners. Add a nose and mouth section from white paper. Use a black marker to draw the nostrils. Glue the nose on to the head.

Cut out two ears from black paper and two horns from white paper.

For the finishing touch and the trademark of great stars, add sunglasses. Use a bright color of construction paper for the frames. Fold paper in half. Cut while the paper is folded for best results. Use dark cellophane for the lens or more black construction paper. Cut two thin rectangles for the earpieces. Glitter or sequins on the frames will add just the right touch of absurdity.

Use book covers, movie posters and magazine covers to finish up the plan.

# READ TILL THE COWS COME HOME

Divide your background into half blue and half green.

A traditional red barn with fences and grass creates a very graphic effect. If you don't want to tackle a three-quarter view of the barn, a much simpler one may be achieved by making a red square. This will work as a front view. Add a triangle to create the roof. Use white chalk to draw on a door. A rectangle can serve as a silo.

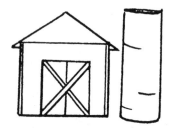

If you are not comfortable making the barn at all, just use sky, grass and a fence. The barn is optional.

Use brown construction paper or brown wrapping paper or even brown grocery bags as the material for your fence. Add some dark lettering and a few book covers and magazine covers.

No cows are needed. Leave them to the viewer's imagination.

Read Till The Cows Come Home.

# TIME TO
# "PIG OUT" ON READING!

The books can be made from construction paper and should be quite large. They will look more graphic if outlined in marker.

The pig really should be made from pink paper. That seems to be everyone's favorite pig color.

The pig is basically only three pieces. The hands can be made by folding a piece of pink paper in half. Draw one hand on the paper. Cut it out while the paper is still folded. By flipping one over, you will now have a right and left hand.

The head can be made by folding a larger piece of paper in half. Draw half of the head on the fold. Cut this out while the paper is still folded.

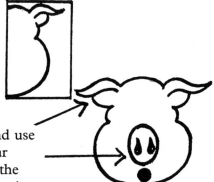

Open out the head and use a marker to draw in the ear lines. Cut a large oval for the snout. Use a marker to trim it.

The mouth is just a circle and can be glued on or done in marker. Same for the eyes.

Use a bold color for the letters and basically any type of background.

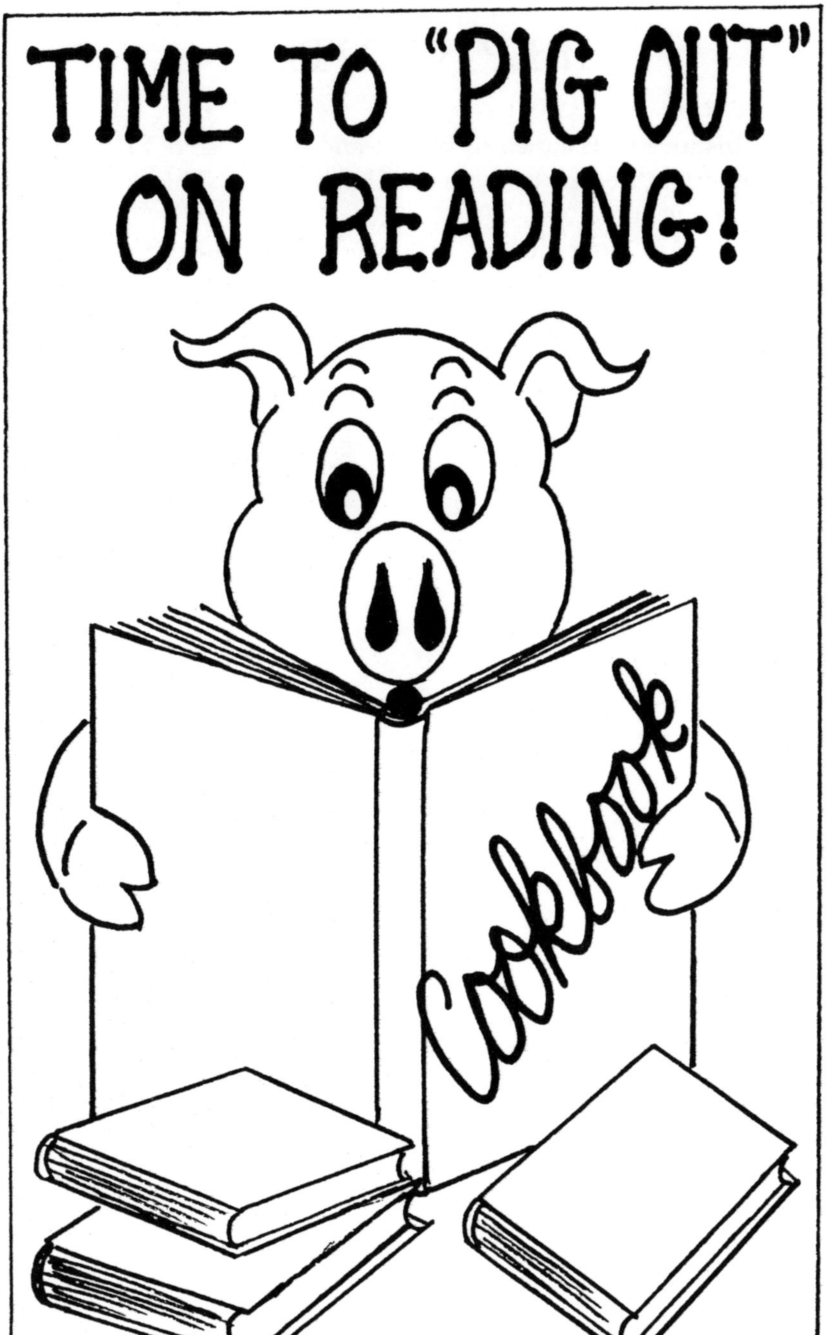
TIME TO "PIG OUT" ON READING!
Cookbook

# HELP WANTED?

This idea is designed to be fast and easy. Use old classified sections from the newspaper as the background. This is to simulate a want ad.

Use black letters for the "Help Wanted?" but use a different color, such as red, for the remaining words. (The old description of a newspaper is "black and white and read all over.") This would be a very appropriate color scheme.

This could fit just about anywhere and could be any size. The format could be horizontal or vertical depending upon your special needs.

# Help Wanted?

THIS LIBRARY CAN HANDLE THE JOB... JUST ASK TO SEE OUR REFERENCES!

# MAKE "TRACKS" TO THE NEW BOOKS

This is relatively simple and would work well in a long, narrow, horizontal space.

Make the letters from blue or red construction paper and make the tracks in black. Use tracks from any type animals or make up some.

Use the track motif throughout the library with tracks or footprints taped on the floor leading the way to a new book display.

MAKE "TRACKS" TO THE NEW BOOKS

# TIME TO GET SERIOUS
# ABOUT STUDYING

Use any type of timekeeping device such as a wristwatch, alarm clock or even a stopwatch. Personalize it for your school.

Use a bold, dark background and a bright color such as yellow for the letters. Keep the watch as simple as possible so as not to detract from the message.

# MAKE TIME TO READ

Any type of clock or wristwatch would work for this bulletin board. Use your school's mascot as the center of attention reading a book, magazine or newspaper.

Use bright, eye-catching colors for the watch. Be bold and try something unusual, possibly even neon colors.

The clock theme or time in general could be featured throughout the library with one o'clock used in the area of the 100's. Five o'clock for the 500's, etc.

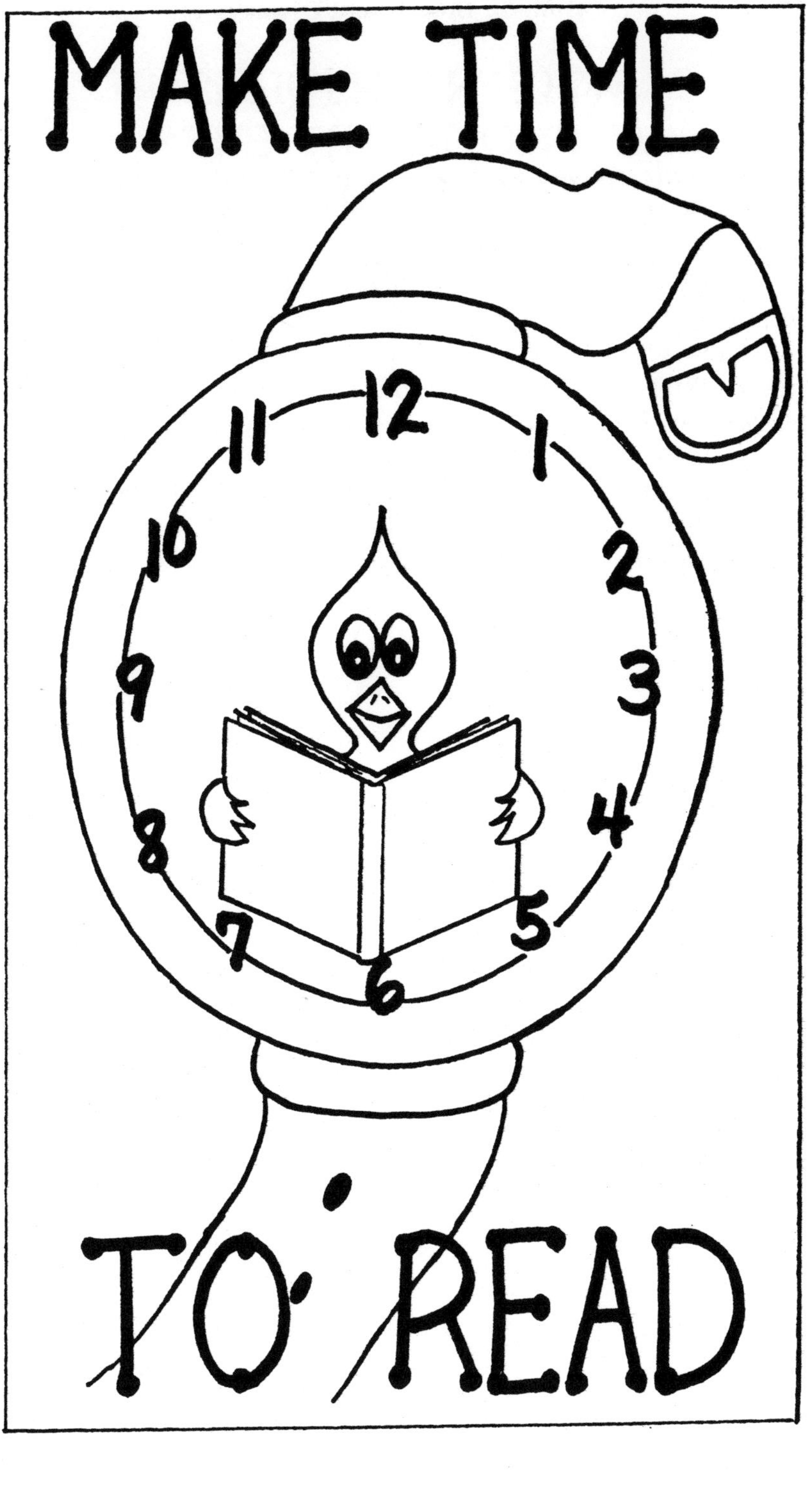
MAKE TIME
12
11
1
10
2
9
3
8
4
7
5
6
TO READ

# THE NIGHT HAS
# A THOUSAND EYES
# FOR READING

The background is a black paper tablecloth. Cut the letters from a light colored paper or foil.

Draw several types of eyes on copy machine paper in black marker. Make several copies of this sheet. This will enable you to easily have many pairs of eyes. Cut other eyes from construction paper and add long, curled eyelashes for a 3-D effect. Glue on roll-around plastic eyes from a craft shop in different places throughout the display to add a little humor.

Use a variety of book covers, magazine covers or newspapers.

# KEEP YOUR EYES
# ON A GOOD BOOK

This display could be made to conform to any size. Use a black background of construction paper, a paper tablecloth, black fabric or even black trash bags opened up. Eyes can be made from white paper and trimmed in black marker. Even glued-on plastic "roll-around" eyes will be effective and will add more humor to the display.

Use white or yellow letters. Add an oversized book that all the eyes seem to be reading.

# SNAP UP A GOOD BOOK!

Use an alligator, dinosaur, snapping turtle or even a mousetrap for this bulletin board. Add some book jackets or books made from construction paper.

For this particular idea, make the alligator from green construction paper trimmed in black marker. A cartoon version is great. Keep it simple and lighthearted.

A dark background is shown here and would be best in a bold blue with yellow or white letters.

# YOU "AUTO" READ ONE OF THESE

Make your own vehicle or cut one out of an advertisement. A particular type of car may appeal to the majority of your patrons. You may even have a student who can make the car for you. This is great, because the more involvement by others, the better.

Any type of background would work, as well as any style of lettering.

Use book jackets or magazine covers for the road.

All types of road signs could be used throughout the library to carry out this theme. Display books on cars, trucks, tips for new drivers and other auto-related topics.

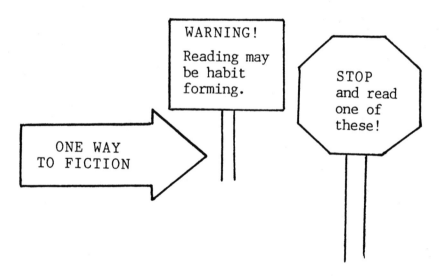

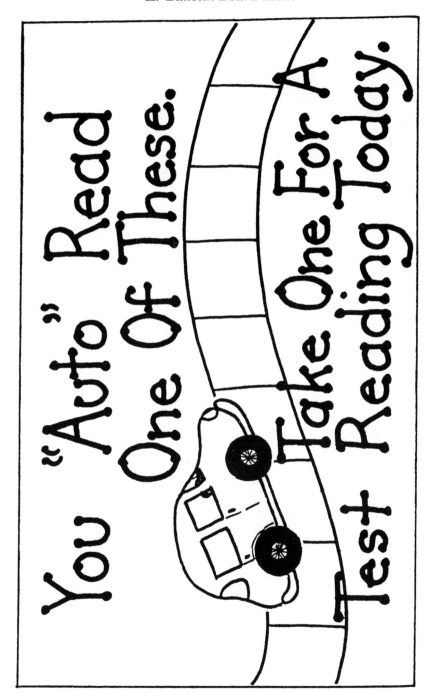

# SO YOU SAW THE MOVIE...

If your bulletin board is horizontal, pretend it is a movie screen. Add construction paper to create the stand.

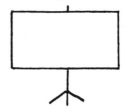

This is a good way to showcase books that are currently out in video. Use book covers or just computer-generate the information about each book to advertise it. Use title, author, call number and other pertinent data. Graphics or drawings will help to make each more attractive.

Use black construction paper or black poster board to create the film frame. Cut holes along the edges to simulate the film sprockets or glue circles of construction paper the same color as the background along the edge of your newly created film.

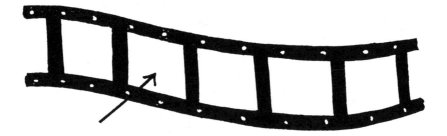

Cut out the squares and insert the book information.

If you have an old 35mm film or some old filmstrips, use them as a border. Stretch the film and pin in place in the sprocket holes.

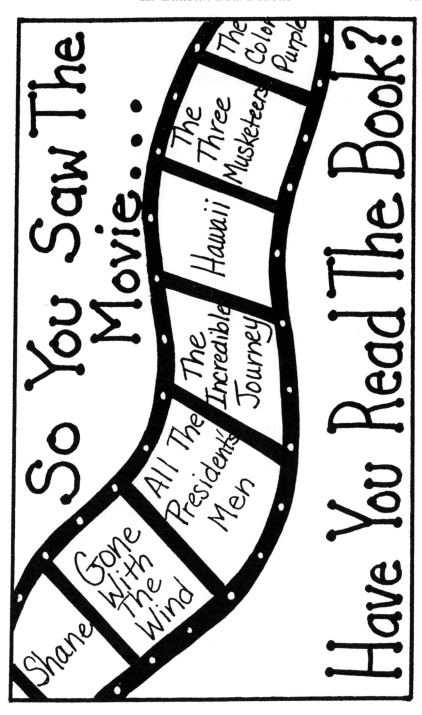

So You Saw The Movie....

Have You Read The Book?

Shane

Gone With The Wind

All The Presidents Men

The Incredible Journey

Hawaii

The Three Musketeers

The Color Purple

# IN THE DOGHOUSE...

Use this on your bulletin board or just use the words on a piece of poster board in conjunction with a display of study helps (see tabletop display idea below).

For the bulletin board, any color background will work. Use a light color for the doghouse. If a three-quarter view doesn't appeal to you, go with the front view. This is just a large square with a triangle added for the roof. Cut out the door, draw it in with markers, or glue one on made from construction paper.

Any color or any breed of dog will work. Actually no dog is necessary. The doghouse is the key.

Cut bone shapes out of light brown construction paper or brown paper bags; basically any color will do. Use a marker to add some possible book titles or subjects that might be helpful to a student hoping to improve low grades.

For a display on the table, make a doghouse out of a box. Paint the box or cover it with paper. Use a large cardboard rectangle folded in half for the gable roof. Attach with duct tape.

Either paint a hole for a doorway or cut one out. Use a toy stuffed dog or use the doghouse by itself.

Display books on study skills and self-esteem.

# GET HOOKED ON READING

This would work for any size or shape bulletin board. Use light blue paper for the water and dark blue or black for the letters.

The fish can be as simple or as complicated as you like. The easiest way is to:

Draw a football shape.

Add some fins and a tail.

Use a marker to draw in eyes, scales and other details.

To make them a little fancier, roll up strips of paper and glue them on for scales.

A second method is to make two fish shapes exactly the same size. Draw the details on in marker, paint or crayon. Staple the two together and stuff with newspapers. This fish will make the total scene seem more three-dimensional.

A more elaborate method is to make the fish out of fabric. Make a newspaper pattern of the basic football shape and then just add fins and tails. Paint on the details or use fabric crayons or markers. These fish can be reused again and again.

Add book covers, magazine covers, seaweed and other aquatic-related paraphernalia. Hang some extra fish from the ceiling in front of the bulletin board.

Get Hooked on Reading.

# READ

This is great for a whole wall or large space. Use student book reviews, book covers, old magazine covers, or even extra catalog cards to spell out the word READ. No background is necessary but, if desired, use a bright, contrasting color.

This is very quick to make and the message is very obvious.

# DON'T GAMBLE
# WITH YOUR GRADES

Use a bold background of yellow or even orange. The contrast of black letters will be attention-getting.

Each card is made from a sheet of poster board. Use regular playing cards for patterns by using an opaque projector to project the image onto your poster board. The ace is the simplest to make and can be used to cover up a part of the second card. This keeps the work on the second card to a minimum. Round off the corners on each card.

Simple cube shapes may be cut from poster board for the dice. Outline the cubes with black marker. Small black circles may be cut from construction paper or the circles could be drawn in with a black marker to finish the dice.

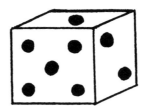

Other types of gambling could be substituted like a roulette wheel or lottery ticket. Use your imagination and consider your patrons as you plan this bulletin board.

# Don't Gamble With Your Grades.

# Use Your Library.

# CATCH UP
# ON YOUR READING

This is a good opportunity to add humor to your decorating.

Use book jackets or books made from construction paper and add legs of any type (even animals') that are on their way somewhere. Bare feet are great, too. Use lots of bright colors and don't worry about realism.

A plain background is good or go all out and make a background of trees, flowers and buildings. Any size will work for this display.

Be wild and crazy!

# READING IS A BRIGHT IDEA IN ANY LANGUAGE!

Showcase languages that are taught in your school. These can then be recognized by your students and the effect will be more meaningful. The foreign language teachers also will appreciate recognition of their subjects.

This plan works well when done in primary colors. Use a light blue background, red letters, red lightning bolts and a bright yellow light bulb.

To construct the light bulb, break it down into two parts. Use yellow construction paper for the bulb. Outline it in black to make it more graphic. Draw in the filament.

Use aluminum foil for the base and outline it in black marker.

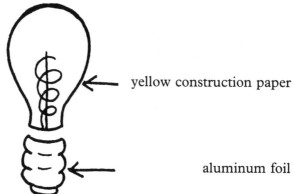

←— yellow construction paper

←— aluminum foil

Cover the finished bulb with clear contact paper. This makes the bulb look more like glass as it will now have a shine.

A border could be made of yellow circles to represent additional light bulbs.

This works well to use with a display of books written in a foreign language or books on learning a foreign language.

*Note:* The following are the words for reading in four different languages: La Lectura (Spanish); Legere (Latin); Das Lesen (German); La Lecture (French).

# PEOPLE WHO READ

Be bold in whatever colors you choose. Solid colors are suggested so that a pattern or design does not detract from your message.

A bold, deep blue is suggested with yellow letters for "People Who Read...." "Succeed" should be in a bolder color such as red or even orange.

Red, blue and yellow are the primary colors and all other colors are made from them. Isn't that what reading is—the primary component for every other learning activity? This is a bold message so be bold in your choice of color and letter style.

People
Who
Read...
SUCCEED

# USING THE LIBRARY IS COOL

Use a flock of penguins to spread the word. This is great for a long, narrow space. Many more penguins could be added to fit your space requirements. Use black and white poster board or construction paper with orange for beaks and feet. Use brighter colors for the books. A blue background with white for snow or ice in the foreground helps to set the mood.

Cut out the black body of the penguin first. Glue on the white for the stomach and the eyes. Cut out beaks and feet. Use a marker for the eyes and to outline the beak and feet.

Use dark-colored letters for the message.

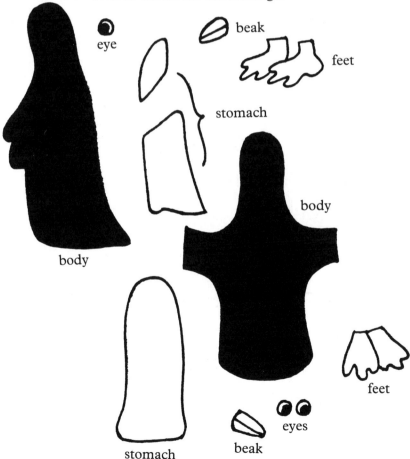

Using the library is cool. Pass it on......

# IN THE NEWS

As you clip the newspapers, look for any photos of your students or faculty members. Designate a display area solely for those photos.

This particular design works well with the background made from half construction paper and half *Wall Street Journal.* Arrange the photos in a pleasing, uncluttered manner.

Change the photos often. Save all the photos in a file till the end of the year. For the final end-of-the-year bulletin board, put up all the photos for the whole year. This will become one of your most popular displays. These can then be put in a scrapbook to be given away, possibly to your school's foreign exchange student.

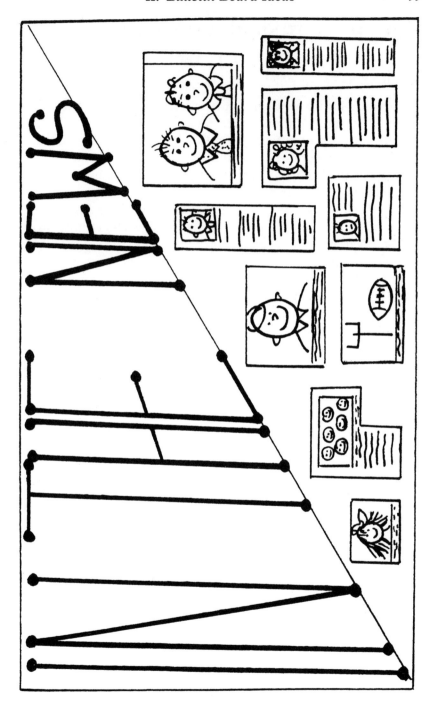

# OUR SCIENCE DEPARTMENT IS ALL ♥

In an effort to spotlight our wonderful faculty, we have begun to feature a different department each month. Photographs of all the teachers in the department are included.

This particular display was done in February—hence the hearts. For the business department, we used the phrase "This Department Is All Business!"

The math department was billed as "Our Super Math Department" while we used "#1 Social Studies Department in the State" to feature the history faculty.

The foreign language department translated the word "terrifico" into the four languages taught at our school (Spanish, German, French and Latin). "Our Foreign Language Department Is Terrifico," etc.

This can be used on a bulletin board or even a window. The main concern to keep in mind is security of the photographs.

Our faculty has enjoyed this little extra bit of recognition.

# DUG UP ANY
# GOOD BOOOOKS LATELY?

This is an opportunity to recycle your tree from the "Have a Tree-mendous Year" bulletin board plan (see p. 12). Use a commercially produced skeleton or make your own. See instructions below.

Use a black tablecloth, construction paper, fabric or several black trash bags for the background. Green, gray or light brown construction paper or newspaper sheets from the *Wall Street Journal* work well for the foreground. Use gray construction paper for tombstones with a book cover or, better yet, a book review by a student attached. Pose the skeleton in a comfortable position reading a good book.

Add a large yellow or orange full moon and spooky letters. To make the letters, just cut them out in a regular way and then cut ragged edges as though the letters might actually be melting.

Skeletons can be made by using white paper plates and white paper. The head is made from one white paper plate. Draw the facial features in black marker. Cut away excess. Use strips of paper cut the same size to form a chain. Use a long rectangle of heavy, white paper for the shoulders. Round off the corners of this rectangle. Form the arms, legs and backbone from the strips of paper made into paper chains.

Trace around your hands and feet or those of a child for a smaller skeleton.

Strips of paper can be stapled in to form the ribs.

The hip bone–pelvis region is made from an additional paper plate with excess cut away.

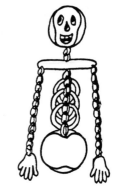

Add paper chain legs and feet.

# NO BONES ABOUT IT

This is a relatively easy Halloween display. For the background, try black construction paper, black fabric, a black paper tablecloth or several black trash bags opened up. Use orange or bright blue for the foreground.

Gray construction paper makes a great tombstone. To make this look even more like stone, spatter it with little drops of black and white paint or make small dots in black and white chalk. If anyone should ask, the RIP stands for "Read in Peace."

Use a purchased skeleton or make the one described in the "Dug Up Any Good Booooks Lately?" plan (see p. 102). Pose the skeleton in a comfortable position reading a good book.

Use white letters on the dark background. Cut the word "bones" in "bone-like" letters. These can easily be made by cutting out your regular letters and then cut these into bone shapes.

The dark letters for BOOOOKS will really stand out against a bright color.

# SEARCHING FOR A SUBJECT?

Use a purchased vampire Halloween-type decoration or make your own. A monster could substitute for a vampire. This would best be used during the Halloween season with an orange background and black letters as the obvious choice.

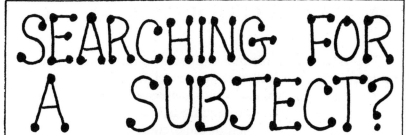

# A DAY WITHOUT READING

This is a very simple bulletin board to make and is most appropriate during the Halloween season. Use a dark background (black is best) with white or yellow letters. Keep the letter style simple for "A Day Without Reading Is." To emphasize "Scary," use fluorescent orange, green or pink letters cut in a ragged fashion. "Scary" should look and give the viewer the definite feeling of being scared!

This display can be done in any size; it can even be done as a poster. It will almost appear to be a public service announcement.

A
DAY
WITHOUT
READING
IS
SCARY!

# BONE UP AT THE LIBRARY

Use the tree you made for "Have a Tree-mendous Year" (see p. 12). Use a large, black paper tablecloth or several black plastic trash bags opened up for the background along with a large yellow construction paper moon.

Purchase a large skeleton or make one of your own (see p. 102 for instructions). A purchased skeleton will easily pay for itself in repeated use.

Photocopy some book covers or use old book covers cut into bone shapes. Use purchased spider webs or make some from stretching polyester fiberfill till it is very thin. Attach the spider webs loosely so that they will move as people walk by.

Cut your letters into bone shapes or just draw bones on your regular letters.

# TURKEY CALENDAR

Thanksgiving bulletin boards often look so out-of-date and boring. Spice up for November with a gigantic turkey holding a calendar of the month's activities. This calendar should include the regular special occasions but really should be primarily of those events unique to your school or city. Throw in a few jokes, riddles or even a left-over turkey recipe.

The turkey is very easy to make. Use an old brown grocery bag for the materials for the head, wings and legs. The head looks like the end of a Q-tip. The beak can be made from orange or yellow construction paper and is a diamond shape finished in marker. Eyes can be cut out and glued on or just drawn on the brown paper with a marker. Use red paper cut in an indefinite shape for the comb and attach beside the beak.

The wings can be cut at the same time from a folded piece of brown paper. This will give you two just alike. The legs can be made in the same way. Finish up with a dark marker.

 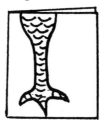

Using bright colors for the feathers, cut the number required to finish the turkey. No particular background is needed.

# WREATH #1

A wreath is a traditional holiday symbol, but one that is very versatile. Wreaths can be made to be any size and out of any type material.

Holly leaves from cardboard, construction paper or tissue paper work well. The cardboard leaves will require a paint job by brush or spray paint. The veins on the leaves can be drawn in with a black permanent marker. Outlining the entire leaf helps to make the display look more graphic.

The beauty of these cardboard leaves is that they can be used again and again, year after year. Construction paper will work well but the leaves are not as durable and will tend to fade if you are planning to reuse them next year.

Red berries can be made by using red paper (foil is great!). Even red Christmas tree ornaments will work nicely for this.

Add a bow and your holiday greeting. Any little extras (like small wrapped gifts) make your wreath just a bit more special.

# WREATH #2

This wreath can be created by arranging book covers, magazine covers, or book reviews in a circle. This could be an opportunity to showcase some special writing by some of your students. Many teachers would jump at the chance to show off some student work. This is great public relations for you and esteem-building for the students.

Be bold in your color choices. Use a contrasting color for the background. Add a bow and a festive greeting.

# WREATH #3

This wreath is great for a low budget. Use brown grocery bags opened up as the material for your gingerbread men and alternate them with book jackets and book reviews. Use a bright red or green background. Be bold in your color choices.

Make a pattern from newspaper by folding the paper in half and drawing on the fold. Open up the pattern and trace around it.

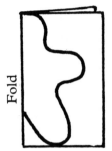 

"Frost" with white paint or white chalk. Add red cheeks, black eyes and black buttons. Finish up with a ribbon bow. Any festive message will work.

Merry
Christmas
To All
And To All
A Good
Book

# MERRY CHRISTMAS TO ALL

This tree could be made up of book covers but would be best made of book reviews. Ask a class or your faculty to write a review of their favorite book. Provide a form for these reviews to be written on so that the pages will all be uniform and displaying them will be much easier for you. Arrange the reviews in a tree shape and decorate with bows, ornaments and other holiday shapes.

Use a bold, bright background of a solid color. Foil paper would work well for this but it is much more expensive. A bold, contrasting color is needed for the letters. Holly leaves make a festive border. Merry Christmas!

MERRY CHRISTMAS TO ALL

AND TO ALL A GOOD BOOK.

# WE  LOVE  READING

Keep everything simple. Use red foil or red construction paper to make the heart. Add lace or net as trim for the heart. Cut out a simple style of lettering. No specific background is required.

This will fit in practically any space.

WE READING

(YOU WILL, TOO!)

# THINK WARM

This works well when used as part of a total theme project for the library. Feature items associated with the tropics or summertime throughout the place. This is terrific to use in January when everyone seems to have those after-the-holiday blahs.

Use a blue background for the sky and brown for the sand. A brown marker can be used to add a few dots of sand. Include a darker shade of blue and add water if so desired. The sun should obviously be yellow but add neon sunglasses and lettering (see below).

The palm tree works well when made from brown mailing paper. Roll this into a long tube and tape the seam. Turn this vertically and pin in place on the bulletin board. If this isn't tall enough, make another one and connect the two. Use a black or brown marker to drawn on some bark-type lines.

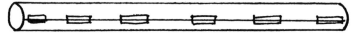

The leaves can be made from green construction paper, poster board or tissue paper. Trim them in marker.

Attach these by twisting them and try to pin them so that they bend and are not flat. You'll want a 3-D effect.

Add a few book jackets or travel magazine covers. Coconuts can be made by balling up a brown lunch bag. Use a marker to add a few circles to simulate the markings on a coconut. These can be pinned in around the palm leaves.

The words "Think Warm" should sizzle. Make them in red, orange or other bright colors. You want people to feel the warmth radiate from your display.

# "HOPPY" SPRING

This is a slightly more elementary type of bulletin board but when used in combination with frog and toad books, books on butterflies, snakes and other nature topics, most secondary students find it is still appealing. You might wish to change from frogs to a setting with kangaroos or grasshoppers.

If possible, use two shades of blue for the background. A slightly darker blue looks better for the water. Everything will look bolder and more graphic if outlined in black marker.

Cut the basic seated frog from a sheet of green paper. To make a pattern, fold a piece of newspaper in half. Cut while paper is still folded.

Trace around this onto the green paper. Add eyes and a large smile. Use a green or black marker to add the darker patches or spots. Add front legs.

The same system will work for the leaping frog.

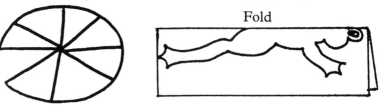

Lily pads are just a circle divided as a pie would be cut with a piece missing. Any color of bold letters will work. Small frogs made from construction paper will add a lot to the book displays throughout the library.

# SPRING HAS SPRUNG #1

Use book covers or magazine covers as centers for large festive flowers.

The flowers could be made from construction paper, wallpaper, tissue paper, really anything. Tuck leaves around your flowers for added color and fullness. Add butterflies, ladybugs, and other spring symbols.

Butterflies could be hung from the ceiling in front of this bulletin board to help with the spring theme. Butterflies are easy to make: 1) fold your paper in half; 2) draw half the butterfly on the fold; 3) cut it out while still folded; 4) use markers to decorate the butterfly.

Cut two thin strips for antennae. Roll them around a pencil for a curly effect. Hang the finished butterfly on a thread or piece of fishing line.

# SPRING HAS SPRUNG #2

This can be done in any size using just about any materials.

A flowered background with solid-colored lettering would work or flowered lettering with a solid background. It also works well to make it a more horizontal composition to fit in a long, narrow space.

Add the springs from green construction paper or use aluminum foil to make them really noticeable. Cut a circle and then begin to cut around and around the inside. The spiral will be formed.

Add flowers, butterflies, book jackets and such for your own spring creation.

An extra touch would be to hang flowers from the ceiling directly in front of your bulletin board. Cut a spiral for them to continue the "spring" theme.

# COMING ATTRACTIONS

As an end-of-the-year countdown of events, this serves as a calendar. Special events are included with a check mark added after the event has occurred.

Emphasize the words "Coming Attractions" by making them larger.

This particular bulletin board was done in primary colors. The background was done in blue, the letters in red and the small circles in yellow to simulate lights around a marquee.

Whatever the color scheme, use bold, vibrant colors because the events are probably very important to your patrons. Color makes a big difference. Bold colors seem to signify importance.

COMING ATTRACTIONS

EARTH DAY . . . . APRIL 22

NATIONAL HONOR SOCIETY ASSEMBLY . . . . APRIL 28

PROM . . . . . MAY 9

AWARDS ASSEMBLY . . MAY 14

JAY DAY . . . . . . MAY 15

GRADUATION . . . . MAY 29

# STILL LIFE

Make large, brightly colored flowers for this giant vase. This was designed to be about six feet tall but could be made any size. Add a message or poem or just use the vase alone. You might ask a class to choose the message for the display.

No background is really necessary. This example is drawn with a dark background to better accentuate the flowers.

The vase can be made from any light color of paper. Light blue works well. Fold the paper in half and draw half the vase on the fold.

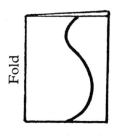

Cut while the paper is still folded. Open it up and use white chalk to draw in the water line.

Shade this upper section in white chalk to make it appear lighter in color. Use a slightly darker shade of blue chalk to shade the bottom section of the vase.

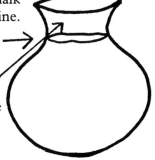

Cut lots of large flowers from pink, orange, yellow, blue or any other color bright construction paper. Use colored chalk or crayons to make them more colorful. Cut green paper stems and leaves. For the stems, glue the construction paper on going from the top of the water up.

Use green chalk to draw the stem as seen through the water. The stem will look slightly distorted by the water.

When attaching the flowers, bend them and twist them so that they stick out and are not all flat against the wall. Try to create some depth and give the whole display some life.

Use flowers in other locations throughout your library. This would be good to use with a gardening display.

# FINISH THE YEAR STRONG

Use construction paper to make all the parts. Start with the books. These can be open or shut or some of each. Front views are the easiest and require only a square. Use the marker to label the book title and to outline the book itself.

Make a pattern for the arms and legs and just make them all alike. They can be posed differently to give some variety.

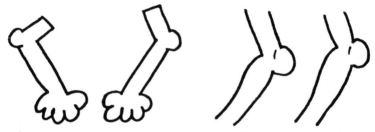

Any type of oversized silly shoes will work but tennis shoes seem the most appropriate for a race. Jagged soles are good with bright stripes, shoestrings, and colorful socks. Use a paper punch to make the shoe eyelets and then use yarn or real shoestrings to add a little more absurdity.

sock

Add a finish line sign or even include the date for the last day of school.

# Part III
# Other Display Possibilities

This section will be devoted to displays that are not for bulletin boards or walls. Displays can be set up just about anywhere, from tabletops to venetian blinds, and can be very simple to extremely elaborate. The subject matter can be of a current newsworthy event such as the Olympics or a presidential election. It can be just a chance to show off some of the library's new books or nonprint materials.

Each area of the Dewey classification system is a possibility for a display. Don't forget to include records, tapes and videos.

**000's** Feature the *Guinness Book of World Records* or books on computers.

**100's** Feature books about witches, ghosts and astrology, or self-help books.

**200's** Mythology books are always popular.

**300's** Feature books on parent/child/family relationships or books on law and our constitution. Books on real or unsolved crimes are very popular.

**400's** How about sign language?

**500's** Feature books on astronomy, dinosaurs, volcanoes, or all types of wild animals.

**600's** Feature cooking books for every cuisine or health and exercise books. Also included in this section are sewing and tailoring books and materials on job hunting and résumé writing.

**700's**  Feature arts and crafts books, music of all kinds and sports books. Feature some old record albums.

**800's**  Use any type of literature, plays or poems, plus humor books.

**900's**  Feature the travel books or the history of a specific country or state that might currently be in the news.

**Biography**  Choose a group of people such as rock stars or baseball players to feature. Time this to coincide with an event like the World Series.

Each of these areas is full of book display potential. Here are some more possible subjects to consider.

- Developing good study skills.
- Comic strips and cartoons—just for laughs.
- Gifts to make for Christmas.
- Car repair.
- Cooking on a diet (including special diets for health reasons).
- Game books or trivia books.
- Short books.
- Long books.
- The classics (or mysteries, science fiction, for example).
- Good grooming.
- Snakes and lizards.
- College—where to go and how to get in, as well as ACT/SAT preparation.
- Fairy tales.
- Unsolved mysteries such as the Loch Ness monster or Bigfoot.
- Public speaking or speech writing.
- Politics and the presidency.
- History and information on your particular state.
- Camping and wilderness books.
- Interior decorating or house design.
- Books by one author. Showcase only one author.

Even the smallest space can be used to convey a message. Cover a few of your metal bookends to call attention to the books in that area or just to make a positive statement about books and reading.

Make your desired sign from construction paper or use a computer-generated sign. Simply tape this on to the metal bookend or create a cover for the bookend.

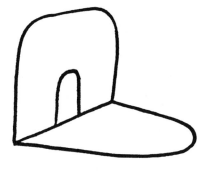

Use bold, bright colors.

To make a cover for the bookend, cut two pieces of paper the same size (larger than the width of the bookend). Staple them together along three sides to create the cover.

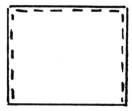

Books can be displayed in many creative ways. Display cabinets are wonderful, but tables, window sills, the tops of books shelves, even cardboard boxes stacked in the middle of the floor, will work as a great location for a library display.

When using a library table, move away all the chairs. This will give you a 3-D display that can be viewed from all sides. A bedsheet or tablecloth will give the table a more polished look ready for the display. A red-checked tablecloth would seem appropriate for a display of cookbooks while a quilt would add a lot to a craft book display.

Small, bendable wire book racks are great for displays and help to protect the books. These are relatively inexpensive. Cardboard ones can be made.

Every display needs a message. The lettering used is extremely important. Sloppy letters equal a sloppy display. Be sure to spell and punctuate correctly.

Letters cut from construction paper can be taped onto the tablecloth or signs on poster board can be suspended from the ceiling. Be sure to use bold colors and keep the message simple.

To make a sign for your display, letters could be cut out and glued onto a strong backing. Computer-generated signs could be used just as well. A piece of sturdy pressed cardboard can be used in the same way picture frames are designed to be freestanding. Even the back of one of these old picture frames will work nicely. (See p. 143 for diagram.)

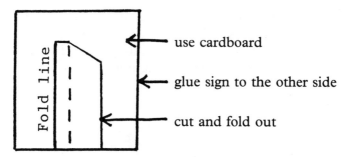

To create some height in the display, cover sturdy boxes with contact paper, wrapping paper, or wallpaper. Stack the boxes up leaving room to set a book or two on all sides. Generally more books can be added to a display using this method and the end result is a more eye-pleasing effect. This is also an opportunity to add more color.

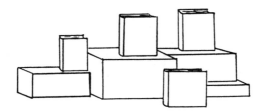

Boxes can also be covered on all sides with posters or pictures to serve as the base for a book display. For example, in a display of books on the Olympics, cover a box with posters of past Olympic champs or use the five-ring emblem. Use this in the center.

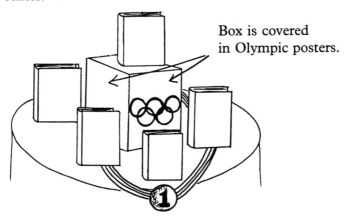

Box is covered
in Olympic posters.

Is there something unusual about your library that you can accent or call special attention to? If there are posts or columns in the room, these can easily become lamp posts, flag poles, candy canes, a turret of a castle, or a multitude of other possibilities.

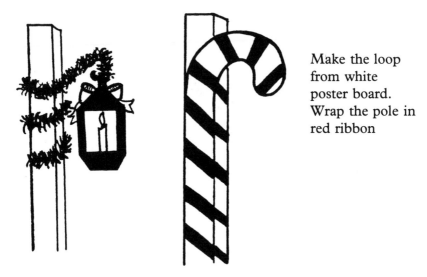

Make the loop from white poster board. Wrap the pole in red ribbon

Always try to add color and festiveness to your library so that it will be the most exciting place in the school. Look around the room for the neglected areas such as the windows or venetian blinds or possibly even the ceiling.

What type of ceiling do you have? The ceiling offers a great out-of-the-way display space just waiting for kites in the spring, hanging leaves in the fall, ghosts or even snowflakes.

Kites in bright cheerful colors can be hung from the ceiling by using fishing line. Many kites are available with extra-long tails and can loop all around your library. This is perfect for March or April. The library might even sponsor a kite-flying event after school just for the fun of it! Display kite-making books and books on topics like origami or even windmills and wind power.

Another spring possibility might be to display the plant and gardening books. Include books on the subject with some real plants, gardening tools, empty flower pots, even some real dirt.

Bricks can be used to elevate some books and still give that out-door look.

Earth Day is now celebrated annually in April. An easy display can be made by using a globe as the central focus of a book display. Elevate the globe by placing it on a box covered by a sheet. Blue is a good color or green which is the color of life or living things. Display books on ecology, the ozone crisis, rain forests, and toxic waste. Hang a sign over the table.

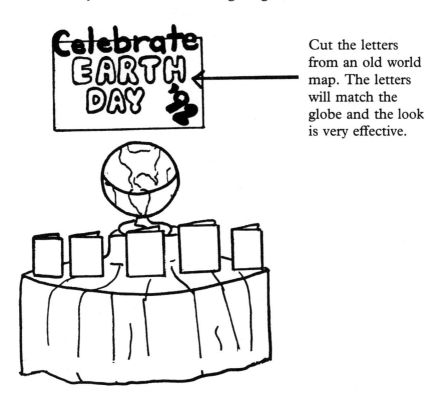

Cut the letters from an old world map. The letters will match the globe and the look is very effective.

Branches from trees are great to use any time of the year. In the spring, a branch in a coffee can works well for an Easter egg tree. Plastic eggs or hand-decorated eggs add lots of color and are cheerful attention-getters. Books from the craft section on egg dyeing or books on Fabergé eggs can be displayed. (See p. 146 for diagram.)

A large branch can be hung from the ceiling to display book jackets, fall leaves, hearts and the like.

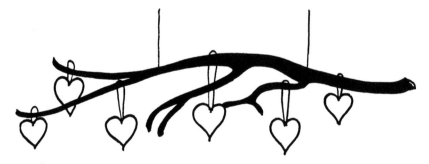

Nature items like large pinecones, cattails, seashells and starfish add a lot to draw attention to books in the science section of your library. Add a fishnet to an area of the library and create a mood for books on fishing, sharks, pirates or underwater adventures or any books such as *The Old Man and the Sea, Sphere,* or *Raising Guppies.* (See p. 147 for diagram.)

Fishnet pinned onto venetian blinds.

Fish can be made from construction paper.

A display like this could fit on top of a bookcase or a table if a window space is not available.

To get attention, why not try a display such as "Books to Read at the Beach" in January. Use a beach poster for the background or make your own beach scene. A beach towel would work well for the base of your display. Add sandpails, sunglasses, sun hats, lotion bottles, sandals, beach balls and even some sand as accessories. Use this same idea for any subject. Go for the unexpected or the opposite of what is normally expected.

Book displays are expected at holiday times. Any pizzazz you add will be appreciated and increase circulation for these books. For Valentine's Day, pull out all those romance stories or poetry books. A table that is accessible from all sides is ideal. With a sheet or tablecloth and a little construction paper, an attractive display is possible at very little cost. Get your heart pumping with a good book!

Add a vase of heart-shaped balloons.

To highlight this display, make this a floor-to-ceiling display by using fishing line.

Attach red hearts with red cellophane centers to the fishing line. The light will shine through the red cellophane.

Use a white sheet topped with a smaller red or pink tablecloth.

Tape on hearts from foil or construction paper.

Halloween is the ideal time to display those scary books that are so popular.

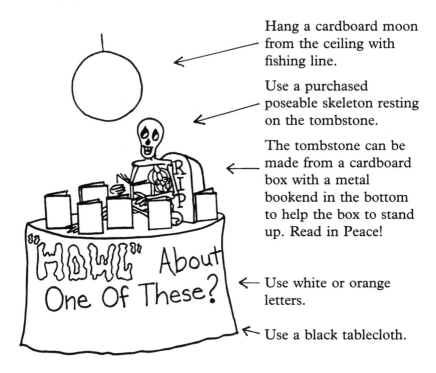

Hang a cardboard moon from the ceiling with fishing line.

Use a purchased poseable skeleton resting on the tombstone.

The tombstone can be made from a cardboard box with a metal bookend in the bottom to help the box to stand up. Read in Peace!

Use white or orange letters.

Use a black tablecloth.

Hang bats and ghosts from the ceiling with fishing line. Black construction paper is easy to use in constructing bats.

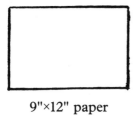

9"×12" paper

Fold paper in half and draw half of the bat on the fold.

<table>
<tr><td>Cut out the bat while<br>the paper is still folded.</td><td>Hang the bat<br>on fishing line.</td></tr>
</table>

Cheesecloth makes terrific ghosts which move with any slight breeze. Bend a coat hanger into the shape shown below. Make sure to bend the ends of the coat hanger back so that no sharp edges are there to poke someone. Sew a casing in the end of one yard of cheesecloth. Slide the material onto the coat hanger. Tack the cheesecloth onto the edges of the hanger or use a small amount of glue from a hot glue gun. Use black material or black construction paper for eyes and a mouth. Hang with a piece of fishing line. Strips of cheesecloth may be attached for arms.

Casing

*Note:* Cheesecloth is often very difficult to work with because it unravels easily.

Cheesecloth is very inexpensive so it is possible to have many ghosts floating around your library. They are also effective because cheesecloth is somewhat transparent.

The size can be adjusted. The bottom can also be tied to create the look of a ghost rising from a small space.

Christmas displays are probably the most fun and the possibilities are endless. One of the easiest is to use a tree branch, which can be sprayed white if desired, stuck into a flower pot full of rocks or into a piece of styrofoam. Decorate this branch like a Christmas tree with small ornaments and bows. This could sit just about anywhere and could serve to showcase some of the beautiful Christmas books that all libraries seem to have.

If your library is on a super-strict budget, just "brown bag" your decorations. Brown lunch bags or grocery bags are excellent to use in making reindeer or gingerbread men.

Cut two antlers from dark brown construction paper. Glue them in where the top of the bag is folded over. Glue on eyes and a gigantic red nose. Add a bow tie or a hair bow for females. These can sit any place in the library and the cost is very minimal.

To make a pattern for the gingerbread man, fold a sheet of newspaper in half. On the fold, draw half of the gingerbread man. Cut while the paper is folded. Open and trace around this on a large brown grocery bag. Use chalk or paint to "frost" the gingerbread man. Draw in the eyes, mouth and other details. Add a ribbon bow.

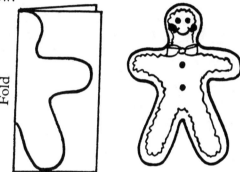

Two gingerbread men can be stapled back-to-back and then placed on the top of a metal bookend. This will allow the gingerbread man to be freestanding.

Another idea which will require more time is to make Christmas banners which each say "Merry Christmas" in a different language. Be sure to start with the foreign languages taught in your school and then add as many as you have time to make. These can be hung from window blinds or from the ceiling.

Use red, green and white construction paper. Aluminum foil and ribbon are perfect for accents.

If you are really industrious, these banners could be made of felt and thereby kept to use year after year. These are lovely and colorful but also educational. This idea can also be done as large Christmas gifts using construction paper with bows and other ribbon added to give a more three-dimensional effect. These can then be displayed on walls or windows or hung from the ceiling.

There are times when an all-out library display will be needed. Everything should be coordinated for the theme and might possibly include a contest to encourage use of the reference books.

A good theme for those cold, dreary winter months is "Think Warm!" To develop a theme such as this, first set the date and think about what would appeal to your patrons most during that time period. Decide just how involved you want to be. Some PR work will be needed to promote the project to your students and faculty. This will be work but the end results will be worth the effort.

With the "Think Warm" theme, use palm trees where possible (see p. 124 for instructions on making palm trees). If your library has support posts, these can be wrapped in brown mailing paper. Green poster board or green construction paper makes great leaves. If no post is available, ask at a local carpet store for the heavy brown tubes from the inside of the carpet rolls. If this isn't an option, roll your brown mailing paper into a long tube for the tree trunks. These can be taped to the wall or tacked onto the bulletin board. About four leaves for each trunk will do. A nice extra touch would be to include a snake or tropical bird.

Add a large sun complete with sunglasses.

From the ceiling, hang a pair of gigantic sunglasses made from poster board. The lens can be made from colored cellophane.

Display books on tropical locations and summertime activities along with beach towels, beach balls, seashells and other beach items. Drag out every type of book, record or tape that has anything to do with being warm. Use travel posters of tropical locations. Ask everyone to wear tropical clothing on a particular day.

Get your students involved by sponsoring a trivia contest featuring questions on warm places, summer recreation, sunburns, the rain forests or even *Gilligan's Island.* All the answers should be found in your library's reference section. Banana split coupons, sun visors and similar items make terrific prizes and might possibly be donated by area merchants or your PTA. You are only limited by your imagination.

Good luck with your displays. They are worth all the effort. Be bold and let your imagination flow and then sit back and soak up all the compliments!

# Index